Weather Around You
Rain

Anita Ganeri

HODDER
Wayland

an imprint of Hodder Children's Books

Weather Around You
Rain · Snow · Sunshine · Wind

Weather Around You – Rain

Text copyright © 2004 Hodder Wayland
First published in 2004 by Hodder Wayland,
an imprint of Hodder Children's Books.

Commissioning Editor: Vicky Brooker   Book Editor: Katie Sergeant
Book Designer: Jane Hawkins   Picture Research: Katie Sergeant
Cover Design: Hodder Children's Books

British Library Cataloguing in Publication Data
Ganeri, Anita, 1961-
   Rain. - (Weather around you)
   1.Rain and rainfall - Juvenile literature
   I.Title
   551.5'77

ISBN 0750245603

Printed and bound in China

Hodder Children's Books
A division of Hodder Headline Limited
338 Euston Road, London NW1 3BH

Cover: Splashing in a puddle in the rain.

Picture Acknowledgements
The publisher would like to thank the following for permission to reproduce their pictures:
Alamy *Contents* (Royalty-free), 8 (Goodshoot); Corbis 6 (Ken Straiton), 7 (Jose Luis Pelaez, Inc.), 9 (Craig Tuttle), 12 (Joe McDonald), 16 (Marc Rebuttini), 17 (Philip Wallick), 18 (Doug Miner), 19 (Bettmann), 20 (James A. Sugar), 22, 23, 24 (Michael Keller); Corbis/ Ecoscene 13 (Chinch Gryniewicz); Getty *Cover* (Photodisc Red/ Royalty-Free), 4 (The Image Bank/ Yellow Dog Productions), 15 (Taxi/ Gail Shumway); OSF 5 (David Cayless), 14 (Dinodia Picture Agency); Science Photo Library 10 (David Nunuk), 11 and *Title page* (Adam Hart-Davis), 21 (Rev. Ronald Royer).

Contents

Words in **bold** can be found in the glossary on page 23.

A rainy day

What do you like doing on a rainy day?
Do you enjoy going outside and splashing
about in the puddles?

Playing in the rain can be fun. We also need rain for water. But too much rain can cause **flooding**. This makes life hard for people and animals.

What is rain?

Rain is made from drops of water. These are called raindrops. They are shaped like circles with flat bottoms. You can see them splashing on the window.

Raindrops can be big or small. Sometimes small drops fall and the rain is light. This is called **drizzle**. But the raindrops in a heavy **shower** are as big as peas.

How does rain fall?

The sun shines on the sea, rivers and lakes and heats up the water. Some of this warm water turns into **water vapour**. It rises up into the air.

As the water vapour rises, it cools down. Some of it turns into tiny drops of water. Millions and millions of drops make a **raincloud**. The wind blows the rainclouds along.

Inside the **raincloud**, the drops of water bump and bash into each other. Lots of them join together to make bigger and bigger drops.

Soon the drops are too big and heavy
to stay up in the air. Then they fall
from the cloud to the ground as rain.

Water for life

Animals and plants need water to stay alive. Farmers use the rain to water their **crops**. If the crops die, people and animals will have nothing to eat.

People need water for drinking, cooking and washing. Some rainwater is collected in large lakes called **reservoirs**. Some is pumped up from underground.

Heavy rains

Some countries, such as India, have months of heavy rain each year. The rain lasts from June to September. It is called the **monsoon**.

Rainforests grow around the **equator**. Here it is warm and wet all year round. The rain is brilliant for making plants grow. Millions of animals live among the plants.

Flood warning!

A flood happens when lots of heavy rain falls in a short time. It can make rivers overflow. Then the water spills over the river banks on to the land.

Floods can be very dangerous. Too much water soaks farmers' fields and spoils the **crops**. It can wash away bridges and roads, and damage buildings.

Living with floods

People try to stop the **flooding** by putting **sandbags** by the doors. They move their furniture upstairs. But if the flood is very bad, they have to leave their homes.

In a flood, the water covers the roads.
Cars and buses cannot drive along.
The only way people can get about is
by boat or air.

Too little rain

A **drought** happens when people expect it to rain but the rain does not come. The land, rivers and lakes dry up. Plants die. People and animals do not have enough to eat or drink.

It is dry for most of the year in the desert. This makes it hard for plants to grow. But lots of seeds lie hidden underground. After a **shower** of rain, the seeds burst into flower.

Rain fact file

- The rainiest place in the world is Mount Wai-'ale-'ale in Hawaii. It rains there for about 335 days every year.

- Arica in Chile has the lowest rainfall. It only gets a trickle of rain each year. Another place in Chile, called Calama, had no rain at all for 400 years from 1570-1971.

- Sometimes, instead of rain, hail falls from **rainclouds**. Hail is made from tiny crystals of ice. The biggest hailstone that ever fell was as big as a melon!

- When the sun comes out after a **shower** of rain, you might see a colourful rainbow. A rainbow is made when the sun shines through raindrops. The order of the colours in a rainbow is: red, orange, yellow, green, blue, indigo, violet. Can you spot them all?

Glossary

crops Plants that farmers grow for food.

drizzle Very light rain with small drops.

drought A time when the land is very dry because very little rain has fallen.

equator An imaginary line around the middle of the Earth.

flooding When water covers the land after a lot of heavy rain.

monsoon A time when very heavy rain falls in countries, such as India.

raincloud A dark cloud which brings rain.

reservoirs Large lakes built by people which fill up with rainwater for drinking and watering crops.

sandbags Sacks that are filled with sand.

shower A downpour of rain.

water vapour When water turns into an invisible gas.

Index